GETTING YOUR EX BACK

Steps to Regaining Lost Relationships

THOMAS PAUL BABADAI

ISBN: 9798847429573

DEDICATION

To Rejoice, Miracle, and Dorcas: If not for the lack of knowledge, all of our fantasies would have come true. Though it is heartbreaking to see that we are no longer together, I hope this book will help us avoid making the same mistakes we did in the past.

To Readers: Much love as you travel down this path of limitless knowledge.

CONTENTS

PART1

1 INTRODUCTION

Thousands of lovers had already separated from their ideal partners (for them) due to relatively clear misunderstandings. It's depressing to consider how frequently these broken relationships would have been wholly averted if both partners had better understood one another's motivations and expectations for the connection.

Sadly, even though men and women are biologically so different from one another, there are specific things that each of us does that might quickly push a partner away rather than keep them close as we'd planned. Then, of course, you could be in pain. Maybe the final stage of your friendship has left you absolutely baffled. However, the truth is that healthy partnerships end frequently and unnecessarily.

Yes, needlessly. Breakups would be unnecessary when both genders were more aware of what the other sex was thinking. In truth, you could have made your connection with your partner into a long-lasting happy union that neither of you would have ever thought to seek elsewhere.

Don't think that everything is gone if you just did break up with the one you assumed had been your dream girl. It's simpler than you think to win back your ex, and there's still hope. Despite trying to tell your ex how much you want to be back together, you may have realised that things aren't going as well as you'd hoped.

The issue is that we don't learn about how the other sex thinks, so for the most part, it is a mystery to most people. So, without ever considering what our spouse might desire in their place, we are stuck trying out strategies that we believe may work.

This book will outline some incredibly straightforward strategies that can help your ex see you in a completely new light and make them fall in love with you all over again.

Do you have the strength of character to reintroduce your ex into your life? Are you prepared for them to love you more intensely and firmly than they did the first time?

Then let's go on to the exciting part.

2 WHEN POSITIVE BONDS TURN NEGATIVE

It's terrible that even the most important relationships can falter from time to time, but there is always a reason, even if we can't see it right away.

In reality, there are innumerable reasons why happy unions fail and end in divorce. For example, your ex may have entirely halted all communications with you before pulling out, leaving you in darkness about what was happening, or you may have endured pointless arguments.

People in pain and unclear about their partner's position in the relationship frequently wind up doing the contrary of what they should be doing to win their ex back.

This is because women tend to try the strategies they would like to see, while men typically act in ways that make sense to them as males. Understanding how men and women think differently is an important lesson. Using female logic to the challenge of gaining back a female typically has the opposite effect, i.e., applying male logic to winning back a guy.

The terribly unfortunate aspect of this is that irrespective of their best efforts, both men and women in these circumstances have the habit of acting in ways that, unknowingly and unintentionally, turn off and push away the person they want to bring back into their life.

This indicates that, although entirely unconscious, they frequently act in a manner that is absolutely at odds with what they should be doing to get their ex back and make them a part of their lives once more. Consider it. Is what you're doing now to gain your ex beneficial? Or is it merely causing you to feel worse by pushing that person further away?

Let's examine a few issues men and women consider in relationships and how they perceive their partner's behaviour. These insights can frequently lead to a much deeper understanding of what might have gone wrong in the relationship and a deeper grasp of what to do when good relationships go awry.

3 Biological Differences Between Men and Women

Individuals could perhaps think this's obvious, but in addition to the evident distinctions, there are crucial hormonal and other biological changes that distinguish us.

For example, do you know men frequently seek strategies to raise testosterone to lower their stress levels? This implies that people will monitor the news after a long day at work to find solutions to start their own "fix it" mode. This presupposes they may enjoy tackling other people's issues because it fuels their desire to strive for solutions to global problems. He may be sitting motionless on the sofa, yet that may be what he is considering. While he manages his stress levels, he will be unavailable to help with real-world issues.

After a long work day trying to prove to their loved ones how wonderful a provider they can be, they will feel much better about the world when their testosterone levels are increased and only attempt to deal with their own troubles after settling down enough.

Unfortunately, women's biological drives are fundamentally different from men's, leading to relationship issues. For instance, when a woman's body contains more testosterone, she may feel more stressed and more inclined to dispute the unimportant problems that her spouse is unlikely to comprehend.

Women will discover strategies to produce the hormone oxytocin to lower stress levels. Oddly, oxytocin is referred to in non-scientific circles as the "petting hormone" and has a solid connection to maternal behaviour and the bonding hormone that encourages a woman to form a stronger attachment with a partner.

Women need to feel loved, adored and appreciated to produce oxytocin. Instead of the hormone testosterone flooding their system, when they think their spouse is retreating from them for any reason, their stress levels rise, and they may become defensive.

Conversely, when a man's hormone levels fall, he will also suffer a similar reaction in which his stress levels rise, becoming more aggressive.

Fascinating stuff, huh?

4 How a Perfect Relationship Can Be Ruined by Hormones

Consider all the times you've been having a good time and are eager to meet your partner. You would have used the day to accomplish things that improved your self-esteem. For example, your levels of the hormone oxytocin may have increased if you were a female and spent some time talking to your girlfriends about different problems you were having to relieve some of your stress.

You would have felt amazing!

However, your ex would have been stressed and agitated after a long day of work when he finished. He has no desire to discuss his issues because doing so would lead his hormone levels to spike with the incorrect hormone. Everything he wants to do is relax, and perhaps while watching TV for a short while, the world's problems can be resolved.

But now that his stress levels are high and possibly even uncontrollable, he is presented with a partner who wants to communicate, share, cuddle, and be loving at this very moment. But unfortunately, he still hasn't had a chance to relax after his demanding day, and now he has dealt with a spouse who appears to be in good health and has no regard for his needs. Do you spot the issue with this straightforward example? If these basic hormonal variations between men and women are not understood, they have the power to ruin even the most vital relationships.

Disillusionment in relationship issues could really happen for a wide range of reasons.

5 When Relationships Fail Due to Other Issues

What happens if you've followed all the procedures, but your ex still avoids you?

There are occasions when relationships fail for no apparent cause at all. For example, your ex may have decided to stop calling you, answer your texts, and entirely withdraw from the relationship even though you thought everything was going fine.

While the completely withdrawing partner may have very different notions about where the relationship was headed in the first place, the rejected partner frequently feels as though they have done nothing wrong.

The truth is that when people fall in love, they secrete a hormone similar to those produced by those with Obsessive Compulsive Disorder (OCD). This is one of the causes of people falling in love, who often find it difficult to focus at work, eat, sleep, or think about anything but the person they are with.

Of course, just because you're experiencing this doesn't guarantee your partner was experiencing it at the exact moment you were. Similar to how not everyone shares the same emotions at the precise moment, they don't all happen simultaneously.

A regrettable aspect of this is that occasionally one of the partners will start to consider moving the relationship forward. They'll take time to reflect on the union's future and imagine various outcomes for the connection once it moves past the initial dating stage.

One may only be attempting to understand their own emotions, but this might cause the other to believe that the connection has developed into something much more profound than it actually has. This is also known as the "instant relationship." While one partner believes they are only dating, the other is in full relationship mode and is perplexed as to why their partner doesn't seem to feel the same way.

The worst thing someone can do in this circumstance is to persuade their partner that they should be together or to convince them of their love for them. When males witness this behaviour in women, it may be enough for them to become hesitant or even want to leave, leaving them to question what is happening. They often distance themselves or withdraw because they perceive their spouse as dependent and hopeless. Men are entirely turned off by a woman who is desperate and insecure.

The truth is that men are guilty of treating the women they admire in the very same manner. As an outcome, they can risk convincing her that he is the only man who can treasure her as much as he does and that he is the best possible match for her. But unfortunately, they don't understand what they're doing incorrectly, which is the difficulty with these circumstances.

6 To Find the Solution, Consider the Beginning.

The key to getting your partner back is always to reflect on the beginning of your relationship.

How did your companion come across when you first met? What was your personality like when you first started dating one another, more importantly?

You were probably both acting properly, making efforts to ensure the other person enjoyed it. Additionally, you would have both been motivated to leave a positive impression on the other person and missed any minor personality or behavioural flaws. Now consider your most recent interaction with your ex. Were you two interacting well with one another? Or did you argue, feel tense, angry, or worried about what the other person was thinking?

If you and your ex were having trouble getting along, this image of you in their mind is likely one of you fighting, being sad, sobbing, and worried about the relationship's future. Thinking joyful ideas about a bright, happy future together is impossible in this situation. Instead, they're probably considering how to meet someone more like the person they initially encountered you as.

The person you existed when you first met, that's correct. However, if you had been a joyful, self-assured, upbeat, motivated, independent person when you first met, they would have fallen in love with you. They would have appreciated wondering when you were free in your busy schedule to see them again because you made them feel joyful while they were with you.

So what changed, then?

7 Errors You May Have Made

Are you guilty of persuading an ex-partner to reconcile their differences and start dating you again? Your intuition may tell you that this person you were meant to spend the rest of your life with, even though your heart may be breaking. Does your ex, however, share your sentiments?

You're probably alienating your ex even more if you've tried to convince them that you're the one for them by calling, texting, emailing, or sending messages. The issue with your frequent contact attempts is that your ex may interpret them as a sign of desperation on your behalf. Nobody enjoys being desperate, male or female. It embodies feelings of inadequacy and emotional neediness, which are highly undesirable qualities in anyone.

Confidence in the opposite sex is incredibly appealing to both men and women. Everyone finds it highly attractive when a person is self-assured, has a clear sense of what they want, and isn't dependent on anybody else to achieve it.

However, someone who suddenly decides that the only way they can be happy is by clinging to you is pretty unappealing. Recall that your partner presumably fell in love with a more upbeat, enthusiastic, and self-assured version of you.

Your ex might have flashbacks to the person they fell in love with because the wretched, lonely, and desperate version of you isn't exactly the same. After all, the miserable person in front of them isn't evoking the same emotions they experienced.

If all you ever heard when you were with someone was their sadness, argument, begging, pleading, or attempts at persuasion, would you feel like you were spending time with a fantastic person? Of course not; you'd want to hang out with more enjoyable individuals, wouldn't you?

Hence, what should you do if you've already slipped into the trap of begging your ex to reach back to you and, as a result, further alienating them? That's what we'll talk about next because, even if you're guilty of calling, texting, emailing, or messaging your ex regularly, it can still be possible to patch up your strained connection.

8 Reversing Old Issues

No matter how considerably you want them to, the first thing you need to do to get your ex back is to not get in touch with them. Texting must end. Put an end to the call. Stop emailing. Do not enquire concerning them from pals; simply quit.

Now, consider your past selves before the meeting. With your own life, you were probably doing great. Your own occupation, friends, and interests would have been your own. Restart them in the same manner as they were before meeting your ex, and get them going once more.

Although you may not feel like it, your depressed emotional state may make you want to stay home and pause for the phone to ring... don't. Preferably, put a smile on your look and interact with your loved ones. Spend time with those who make you feel positive about yourself and your interactions with them.

Do not associate with someone who will encourage you to feel depressed over your broken heart. Make sure to avoid them because they won't do anything to aid in your quest to win back your ex. The trick here is to reclaim the joyful, self-sufficient version of yourself that first attracted your ex.

After a while, your ex will start to wonder why you haven't called or communicated with them, and they'll start worrying about you. Even if you aren't there yet when this occurs, you will have made progress. Consider this: worrying for you suggests that your ex still has some amount of concern for you.

The big lesson is to stop reaching out to them and focus on what's happening inside you instead.

PART 2

9 Getting Rid of the Fairy-Tale View of Relationships

Hollywood films are essentially to blame for the fairy-tale images of love that most people have in their heads. Somehow, the silver screen has convinced us that after much acting, fighting, and debating, the beloved of our lives will unexpectedly come to their senses, and we will all live happily ever after.

This is unrealistic and is more likely to occur in romantic romance films than in real life. The truth is that your ex is not the key to achieving happiness. You certainly are.

You don't have to be with another person to be happy or fulfilled. You only need yourself and your personal interests, hobbies, passions, and things that make you happy.

You were probably happy, independent, and confident when you first met your ex. These are highly appealing characteristics to the opposite sex. So get out there. Have a good time. Spend time with your friends. Watch silly comedies that don't make you think about them or make you angry. Purchase a new outfit, and get a new hairstyle. Work out for a while. Spend time grooming and pampering yourself.

When you look nice, you feel fine, and when you feel fine, you become more appealing to those around you. Your confidence will naturally return, and you'll soon discover things to be happy about all around you. This strategy serves another purpose.

It will not only help you get over the fact that you broke up with your ex, but it will also help you reconnect with the person you were when your ex first encountered and sank in love with you.

10 Getting in Touch with Your Ex Again

You'll start feeling better after you've spent some time restoring your confidence to where it was before you met your ex. You'll also be better positioned to reconnect with your ex.

When you stop contacting them, it's sometimes enough to make them want to pick up the phone and call you to check on you. If they have done this, you know they still care about you but don't meet too soon. Before doing this, ensure you feel more like your old happy self.

However, if they haven't called and you've been working on your self-esteem for a couple of weeks, you might want to try a friendly phone call just to say 'hi'. Don't insist on discussing the relationship, and don't invite them out for coffee. Instead, simply tell them you want to say hello. This will allow you to start a conversation about what you've been up to in the weeks since you split up. Inform them that you've been out, having fun, and doing things for yourself.

It's also acceptable to 'let it slip' that you've been thinking about them sometimes, but don't let the initial conversation become too involved with the connection or the breakup. This is very significant.

Also, before you conclude the discussion, mention that you'd like to catch up at some point.

However, do not suggest a time or location.

11 Playing the Want game, not the Get game

It's no secret that men have a penchant for pursuing what they believe they can't control. Unfortunately, numerous women take this too far and start dating someone new just to make their ex jealous. This is never successful. By quickly moving on to another guy, you'll tell him that your relationship wasn't necessary to you and that you've already moved on. Even though he still has feelings for you, he won't act on them.

Playing hard to get simply means remembering not to drop everything you're doing and rush to them the moment they call. Instead, let the ring go to voice mail and call back when you're in a good mood.

If they propose a date, you can accept it as long as you change the proposed date. For example, they might want to meet for coffee on a Friday. So agree to meet for coffee, but inform them that you will be too busy on Friday and that Saturday would be a better time.

Call a pal and see a movie; don't matter what else you're up to on the suggested day. Just make sure they understand you're preoccupied. If they want to be a component of it again, they will have to put in some effort to get your attention.

When you meet up with them again, schedule another meeting ahead of time, so you are forced to be on a time limit. Explain that you won't be able to stay long and must leave at a specific time. This will most likely result in you cutting your conversation short, and if you've enjoyed each other's company, they will undoubtedly want more.

After your first meeting, resist the urge to call them immediately to set up another date. Instead, allow a few days to see if they contact you first.

Remember that they have images in their head of the reasons you broke up. One meeting with you as your old self will not be enough for them to forget the problems that separated you. If you genuinely want those feelings back, you must spend time rekindling them for yourself.

But be wary of your tactics when playing hard to get. You don't want to be one of those challenging people to enjoy. These are the people who cross the line from confidence to arrogance. They have strong opinions and are willing to express them, even if it means starting fights. However, they are adamant about being utterly blameless in the breakup of the relationship, and they accuse their ex of everything that moved bad.

If you think negatively while out with your ex, be prepared to leave the date and get out while the going is good. If you don't, you risk permanently losing them.

12 Getting Your Ex to Love You Once More

Consider this: your ex met you and felt a strong attraction to you. The better moment you spent concurrently, the more powerful his feelings would have become. Then something drove incorrect, and the relationship ceased. They may say they don't feel the exact way anymore or have simply disappeared into the distance, refusing to call or respond to your messages.

Even if the fire has been extinguished, you can bet there will be embers in the back of their mind. It's your job to fan those embers into a spark and rekindle them. If you're serious about getting your ex back, you'll need to discuss what went wrong in the relationship and why it ended. Just make sure you don't do it too soon.

After an emotional breakup, you need time to process your feelings and figure out what happened. Of course, you mustn't bring up the subject of the separation during that first meeting when you see your ex after a long time apart. Instead, allow them to see the happy, confident version of you they fell in love with from the beginning.

Some individuals may be interested as to why you did not try to persuade them to return, demand to know why they left, or do anything else they would do in that situation. This curiosity often makes them pick up the phone and ask for another date just to see what you'll do next.

Of course, some people will conclude that you must be playing a mind game and will continue to avoid you. If your ex is one of the latter, wait a week after you've met before calling to set up another friendly meeting.

While these strategies may appear simple, they are intended to keep your ex thinking about you when you are not present. The more they think of you when you're apart, the more likely they'll want to call you again.

13 Reestablishing a Stronger Bond

It is pointless to wish for your old relationship to be rekindled. After all, your relationship is over. It was ineffective. You don't want to mend a shattered relationship. Instead, you should focus on constructing a new relationship version, but this time on a much firmer foundation.

Consider the things you liked best about your previous relationship before it ended. Then, consider some parts you know could cause problems or make you unhappy. Be very selective about which aspects you want to bring into your new relationship with your ex and which you want to leave behind.

When you've reestablished contact with your ex and are starting to date regularly, it's time to speak concerning what stirred wrong in your last relationship. If your ex is unwilling to talk about it, let it go until they are. After all, if you're playing 'hard to get,' they should start looking for ways to get your attention to find the right time to discuss what went wrong.

Instead of asking what went wrong, try asking what they would prefer to see done correctly. This gives them a legitimate opportunity to use their problem-solving skills and find ways to strengthen their bond. Focusing on the positive aspects of what you both want to enjoy in your relationship can be a relaxed way of dealing with a sensitive issue and turning it into something fun for you.

If you focus on past problems or the negative aspects of the breakup, you may find that your conversations return to negative territory. You bear the chance of sparking controversy in this manner. Instead, concentrate on the positive things you can both do.

It is much easier to rebuild your new relationship on a solid foundation when you both have a clearer understanding of how you want it to be.

14 Too Fast, Too Soon

Many people automatically assume that if you're dating your ex again, you're back in a relationship. Your partner, on the other hand, may not think so. Dating is simply spending time together, going out, and doing things you enjoy, but it is not a relationship. No, not yet.

Don't make assumptions about their thoughts or feelings unless they specifically tell you. This also means you shouldn't ask when they think you'll be able to get back together, or you'll end up looking like the desperate person they already pushed away. Instead, keep having fun together. Dates should be scheduled. Make sure you're both maintaining a good time. Throughout it, all, make sure you're not the one who drops everything when they call or want to go out.

Even if getting your ex back is your primary goal, you must prioritise your personal life. After all, when you're not with your ex, your friends, family, work, hobbies, and interests define you. They are essential to you and help you maintain your confidence and reduce stress.

Let them know when you're unavailable for a date and have other plans. You want them to pursue you until you know their feelings for you are growing. Then, it won't be long before they're the ones asking if the relationship is still going on.

15 Being Happy Again

If you've managed to entice your ex back into your life, ensure you're not hiding who you indeed are. People can learn little tricks to get people to fall for them so that they will act or say certain things to maintain their interest. The issue with working this way is that you are not being yourself. Who is your partner really falling for if you're not being yourself? And what will they think of you when you stop acting and start being yourself again?

If you're serious about repairing your relationship with your ex, resist the temptation to use tricks, mind games, or silly tactics to make people love you. Instead, simply be yourself. . You recall - the confident, playful, and fun-loving person they admire.

Be the best possible version of yourself. Maintain a positive attitude, look for the good in people, and seek ways to bring happiness into your life. Have fun with your friends and hobbies or interests. Look and feel your best, and your self-assurance will shine through.

After all, was said and done, your ex fell in love with you when you first met. They will most likely still love you for who you are. So make them fall in love with you all over again.

Also, best wishes!

ABOUT THE AUTHOR

Thomas Paul, known as "The Relationship Expert," is an 8-year-old relationship therapist and coach. He is also the founder of a community-based initiative, where he impacts lives in rural communities, adding to his coaching passion for relationships. Paul has an impressive resume and has guided people worldwide through the ups and downs of dating. Paul teaches his clients how to heal their past, unconditionally love themselves, be vulnerable, tap into their inner strengths and intuition, and live more authentically to achieve their relationship goals. In addition, Paul helps his clients realise that they were born to have love in their lives, not just any love - but the kind that lives life enjoyably while bringing peace to the soul.

What distinguishes this book is that each detail stems from a personal experience.

www.ingramcontent.com/pod-product-compliance
Lightning Source LLC
LaVergne TN
LVHW020530160826
845677LV00015B/3989

* 9 7 9 8 8 4 7 4 2 9 5 7 3 *